Foreword.

This volume is a sequel to our previously published and now widely used Easy Classics To Moderns and More Easy Classics To Moderns (Numbers 17 and 27 in the Music for Millions Series). The piano literature of nearly three centuries is represented by these original compositions of medium grade difficulty. All selections are in their original form, neither re-arranged nor simplified. They are set in approximately chronological order.

# CLASSICS TO MODERNS

*In The Intermediate Grades*

*Compiled and Edited by Denes Agay*

Marks of phrasing and expression are often editorial additions especially in the music of the pre-classical period. These signs were added for a quicker and easier understanding of the structure and mood of the compositions. They are to be considered as suggestions rather than rigid directions. Students, teachers and all pianists should find these original piano works valuable for study, recital, sight reading or just inspired musical entertainment of the highest caliber.

The Publisher.



Order No. AM 41617
International Standard Book Number: 0.8256.4037.7
Library Of Congress Catalog Card Number: 62-22540

*Exclusive Distributors:*
Music Sales Corporation
257 Park Avenue South, New York, NY 10010 USA
Music Sales Limited
8/9 Frith Street, London W1V 5TZ England
Music Sales Pty. Limited
120 Rothschild Street, Rosebery, Sydney, NSW 2018, Australia

Printed in the United States of America by
Vicks Lithograph and Printing Corporation

**Amsco Publications**
New York/London/Sydney

# Contents

ABOUT STRANGE LANDS AND PEOPLE ........ Robert Schumann 84
ADAGIO *from Toccata No. 11* ........ Georg Muffat 10
AIR ........ Henry Purcell 4
ALBUM LEAF ........ César Franck 103
ALLA POLACCA ........ Carl Philipp Emanuel Bach 54
ALLEGRO (A Major) ........ Wilhelm Friedemann Bach 50
ALLEGRO GIOCOSO (F Major) ........ Joseph Haydn 64
ALLEGRO SCHERZANDO ........ Joseph Haydn 58
ALLEMANDE (A minor) ........ Georg Friedrich Händel 35
ARIA ........ Johann Kuhnau 20
BAGATELLE (Op. 119, No. 11) ........ Ludwig van Beethoven 71
BAGATELLE (Op. 119, No. 5) ........ Ludwig van Beethoven 72
BALLET ANGLOIS ........ Johann Kaspar Ferdinand Fischer 11
BOURREE I *from French Overture* ........ Johann Sebastian Bach 33
BOURREE II *from French Overture* ........ Johann Sebastian Bach 34
BRISK GAME ........ Dmitri Kabalevsky 136
CANZONI DI DANZA ........ Bernardo Pasquini 12
CAPRICCIO ........ Domenico Scarlatti 18
CHACONNE (G Major) ........ Georg Friedrich Händel 40
CHANSON SANS PAROLES (Op. 40, No. 2) ........ Jan Sibelius 130
CHILDREN'S PIECE (Op. 72, No. 1) ........ Felix Mendelssohn 90
COURANTE (F Major) ........ Georg Friedrich Händel 37
COWHERD'S SONG, THE *from Op. 17* ........ Edvard Grieg 108
DANCE WITH A BELL ........ Vladimir Rebikoff 127
DAWN ........ Béla Bartok 160
ELFIN DANCE ........ Edvard Grieg 110
FANTASIA (D Major) ........ Carl Philipp Emanuel Bach 53
FANTASIE (G Minor) ........ Georg Philipp Telemann 43
FARMER'S DAUGHTERS ........ Heitor Villa-Lobos 146
FIVE ECOSSAISES ........ Franz Schubert 80
FOUR HUNGARIAN FOLK TUNES ........ Béla Bartók 155
1. COURTING SONG ........ 155
2. PLAY TUNE ........ 156
3. STARS, SHINE BRIGHTLY ........ 158
4. DRINKING SONG ........ 159
FROM A STORY BOOK ........ Robert Volkmann 112
FROLIC (Op. 17, No. 12) ........ Max Reger 124
FUGHETTA ........ Domenico Zipoli 13
FUGHETTA (G Major) ........ Johann Sebastian Bach 30
FUN AT HOME *from "The Adventures of Ivan"* ........ Aram Khatchaturian 148
GAVOTTA ........ Arcangelo Corelli 14
GAVOTTE *from French Suite No. 5* ........ Johann Sebastian Bach 32
GERMAN DANCE (G Major) ........ Joseph Haydn 60
GIGUE *from Suite No. 11* ........ Georg Friedrich Händel 42
GIGUE EN RONDEAU ........ Jean Philippe Rameau 48
GOODNESS! ........ Heitor Villa-Lobos 147
GYMNOPEDIE NO. 3 ........ Erik Satie 134
HORNPIPE ........ Henry Purcell 6
HORSEMAN, THE ........ Dmitri Kabalevsky 140
IMPROVISATION ........ Robert Schumann 87
INTERMEZZO ........ Theodor Kirchner 107
INVENTION (C Major) ........ Johann Sebastian Bach 28

IVAN IS ILL *from "The Adventures of Ivan"* ........ Aram Khatchaturian 150
JIGG ........ Jeremiah Clarke 8
JUGGLER, THE ........ Johann Philipp Kirnberger 55
KAMARINSKAIA (Russian Folk Tune) ........ Peter Ilyitch Tchaikovsky 104
KUKLA (The Russian Doll) ........ Vladimir Rebikoff 128
L'AUGUSTE ........ Carl Philipp Emanuel Bach 51
LA DIANE ........ Francois Couperin 21
LA FLORENTINE ........ Francois Couperin 22
LA JOYEUSE ........ Jean Philippe Rameau 46
LAMENT ........ Zoltán Kodály 154
LITTLE PRELUDE (C Minor) ........ Johann Sebastian Bach 26
MARCH *from Suite No. 5* ........ Henry Purcell 7
MAZURKA (Op. 67, No. 2) ........ Frédéric Chopin 98
MENUETT ........ Gottfried Heinrich Stölzel 24
MINUET (C Minor) ........ Joseph Haydn 62
MINUET AND TRIO *from Viennese* ***Sonatina No. 1*** ........ Wolfgang Amadeus Mozart 68
MUSETTE *from English Suite No. 2* ........ Johann Sebastian Bach 39
NORSE SONG ........ Robert Schumann 85
NOVELETTE ........ Dmitri Kabalevsky 138
ON THE PLAYGROUND ........ Nikolai Rakov 152
PARADE OF THE GRASSHOPPERS ........ Serge Prokofieff 143
PASSEPIED ........ Georg Philipp Telemann 38
POLKA ........ Peter Ilyitch Tchaikovsky 105
POLONAISE ........ Wilhelm Friedemann Bach 59
PRELUDE (Op. 28, No. 6) ........ Frédéric Chopin 94
PRELUDE (Op. 28, No. 7) ........ Frédéric Chopin 95
PRELUDE (Op. 28, No. 4) ........ Frédéric Chopin 96
PRELUDE (Op. 28, No. 20) ........ Frédéric Chopin 97
PRELUDE (Op. 11, No. 4) ........ Alexander Scriabine 129
PRELUDE ........ Dmitri Shostakovich 142
ROMANCE ........ Reinhold Glière 132
RUSTIC SONG ........ Robert Schumann 86
SAEBYGGA (Song of the North) ........ Edvard Grieg 109
SARABAND *from Suite No. 2* ........ Henry Purcell 5
SCHERZO ........ Johann Nepomuk Hummel 88
SEA PIECE (Op. 55, No. 5) ........ Edward MacDowell 120
SIX VARIATIONS ON A SWISS SONG ........ Ludwig van Beethoven 74
SOLFEGGIETTO ........ Carl Philipp Emanuel Bach 56
SONATA (G Major) ........ Domenico Scarlatti 15
SONG OF THE NORTH (Saebygga) ........ Edvard Grieg 109
SONG WITHOUT WORDS (Op. 19, No. 4) ........ Felix Mendelssohn 92
TARANTELLA ........ Michael Glinka 100
THREE LÄNDLER ........ Franz Schubert 78
THREE WALTZES ........ Franz Schubert 82
TO A WILD ROSE *from "Woodland Sketches"* ........ Edward MacDowell 118
TOCCATA ........ Leonardo Leo 16
TRIO *for Menuett by Stölzel* ........ Johann Sebastian Bach 25
TWO BRAZILIAN CHILDREN'S SONGS ........ Heitor Villa-Lobos 146
VALSES POETICOS ........ Enrique Granados 114
VIENNESE SONATINA NO. 1 (*First Movement*) ........ Wolfgang Amadeus Mozart 66
WALTZ (K. 567, No. 5) ........ Wolfgang Amadeus Mozart 70
WALTZ (Op. 39, No. 9) ........ Johannes Brahms 102
WALTZ (Op. 39, No. 8) ........ Peter Ilyitch Tchaikovsky 106

# Air

Henry Purcell
(1659-1695)

# Saraband

Henry Purcell

# Hornpipe

**Allegro**

Henry Purcell

# March

Henry Purcell

**Moderato**

# Jigg

Jeremiah Clarke
(1669–1707)

dim.
p
mf
p
cresc.
dim.
mf
f
rit.

# Adagio

from Toccata No. 11

George Muffat
(1645–1704)

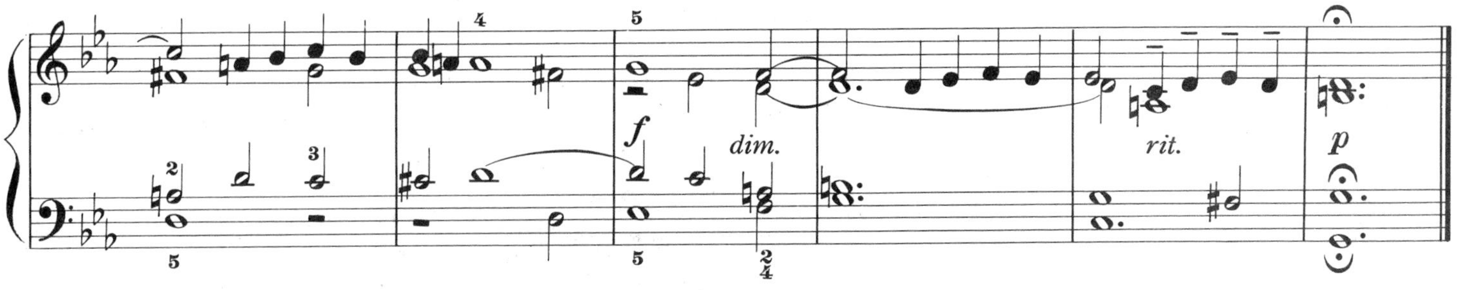


# Ballet Anglois

Johann Kaspar Ferdinand Fischer
(1650–1746)

**Allegro giocoso**

* *Play all eighth notes staccato*

# Canzoni di Danza

Bernardo Pasquini
(1637–1710)

**Vivo; energico**

**Allegro**

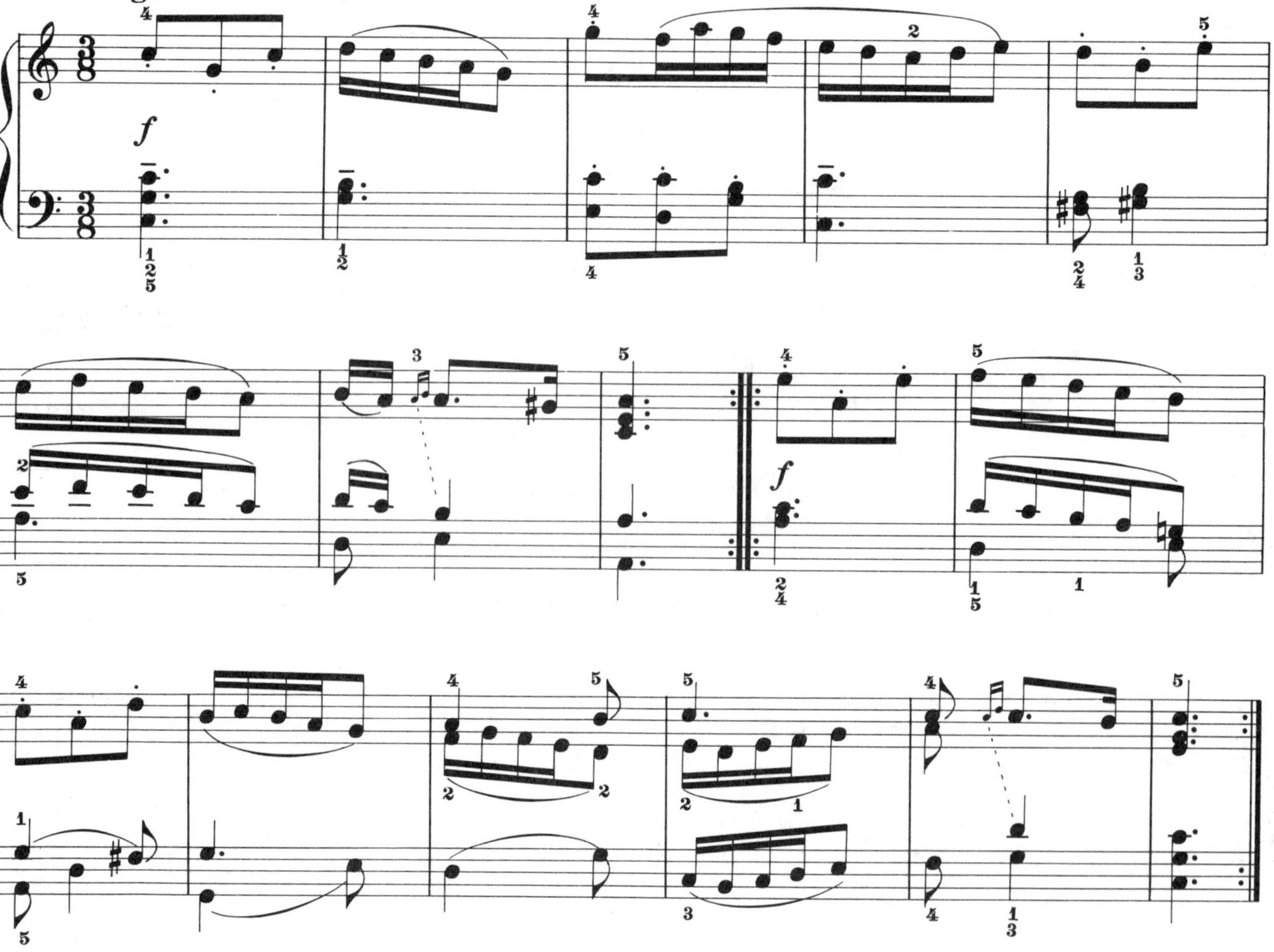

* *Play all eighth notes staccato*

# Fughetta

Domenico Zipoli
(1688-1726)

**Allegro energico**

# Gavotta

Arcangelo Corelli
(1658-1713)

# Sonata

Domenico Scarlatti
(1685–1757)

# Toccata

Leonardo Leo
(1694-1744)

f
p
crescendo
mp
crescendo
f
p subito
f
mp
crescendo
allargando
f

# Capriccio

Domenico Scarlatti
(1685-1757)

**Allegro moderato**

f
p
f
p
mf
p
cresc.
f

# Aria

Johann Kuhnau
(1660–1722)

**Andante cantabile**

# La Diane

Francois Couperin
(1668–1733)

# La Florentine

Francois Couperin

* *Original time signature* $\frac{12}{16}$

poco rit.
a tempo
p

# Menuett

From J. S. Bach's "Little Note Book
for Wilhelm Friedemann Bach"

**Allegro giústo**

Gottfried Heinrich Stölzel
(1690 - 1749)

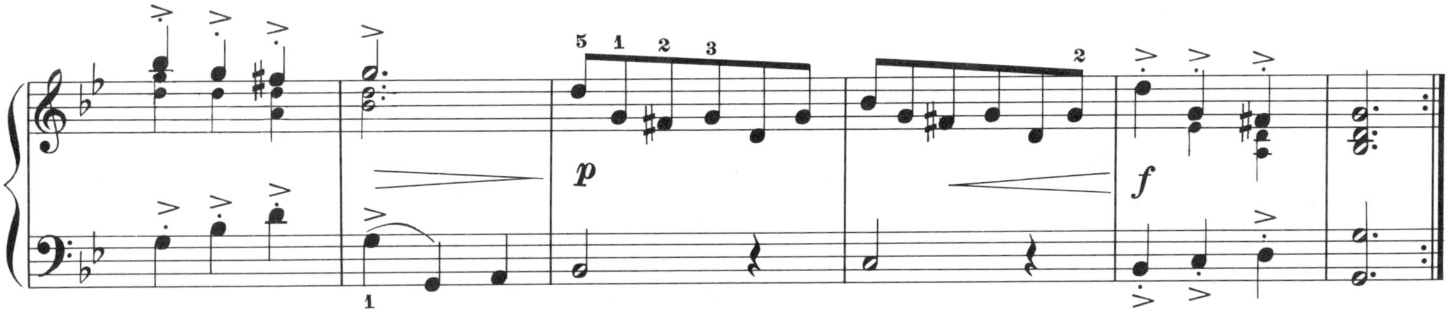


# Trio*

Johann Sebastian Bach

(1685 - 1750)

**Andantino espressivo**

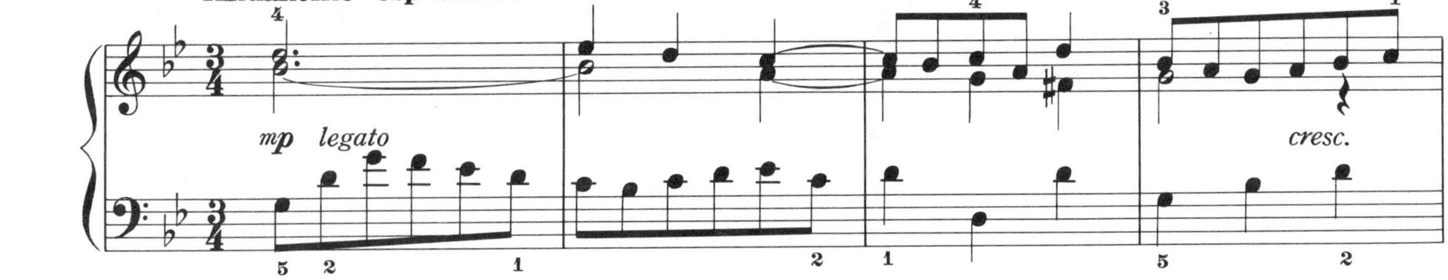


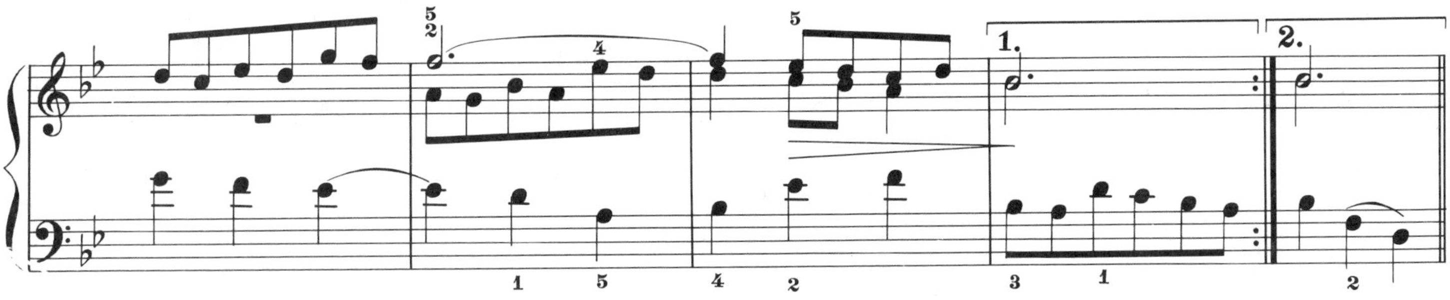

*Repeat Menuett*

* *Bach wrote this Trio to follow and be part of the preceding Menuett*

# Little Prelude

**Con moto**

Johann Sebastian Bach

mf
dim.
p
cresc.
f

# Invention

Johann Sebastian Bach

più f
crescendo
f
p
crescendo
f
poco rit.

# Fughetta

Johann Sebastian Bach

**Allegretto**

f
L. H.
rit.

# Gavotte

from French Suite No. 5

Johann Sebastian Bach

**Allegretto**

# Bourrée I

from French Overture

Johann Sebastian Bach

# Bourrée II

from French Overture

Johann Sebastian Bach

**Allegro cantabile**

## Allemande

Georg Friedrich Händel
(1685–1759)

**Andante**

mf
dim.
p
cresc.
f
p
f
dim.
cresc.
rit.

# Courante

Georg Friedrich Händel

# Passepied

Georg Philipp Telemann
(1681-1767)

**Vivo**

# Musette

from English Suite No. 2

Johann Sebastian Bach
(1685-1750)

**Andantino grazioso**

# Chaconne

## Theme And Six Variations

Georg Friedrich Händel

**Andante**

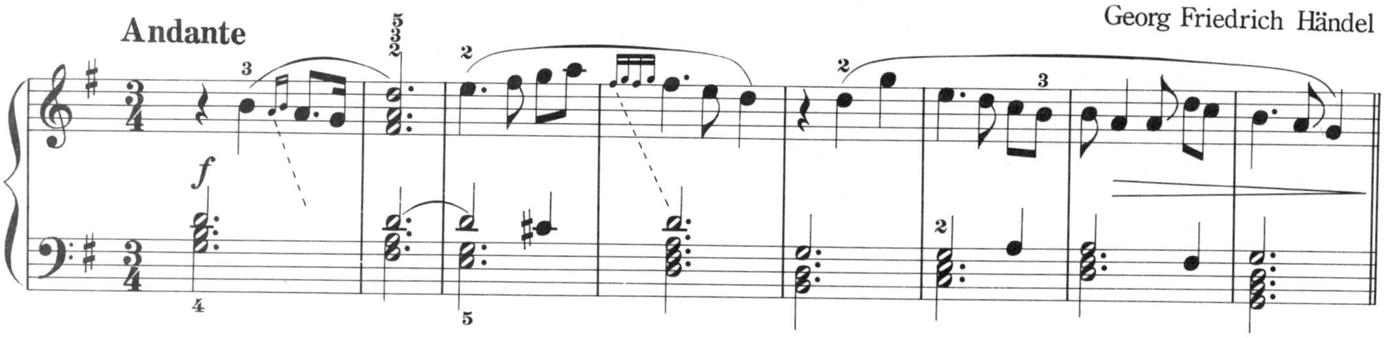


Var. 1

**Poco più mosso**

Var. 2

Var. 3

dim.
Var. 4
f pesante
Var. 5
p
cresc.
mp
dim.
p
Var. 6
f
sempre f
rit.

# Gigue

Georg Friedrich Händel

# Fantasie

Georg Philipp Telemann
(1681-1767)

**Vivace**

p
legato
mf
p
f
p
f
mp cantabile

p subito
crescendo
f
allarg.
a tempo
f
mp
f
allargando
ff

# La Joyeuse

Jean Philippe Rameau
(1683-1764)

**Giocoso**

mf
f
p
mp
p
crescendo
f
poco rit.

# Gigue En Rondeau

Jean-Philippe Rameau
(1683–1764)

Fine
p
crescendo
f
mf
dim. sempre
p
D. S. al Fine

# Allegro

Wilhelm Friedemann Bach
(1710–1784)

D.C. al Fine
(senza replica)

# L' Auguste

Carl Philipp Emanuel Bach
(1714–1788)

**Andante cantabile**

p
crescendo
mf
p
f
R.H.

# Fantasia

Carl Philipp Emanuel Bach
(1714–1788)

# Alla Polacca

Carl Philipp Emanuel Bach

**Moderato**

# The Juggler

Johann Philipp Kirnberger
(1721-1783)

# Solfeggietto

Carl Philipp Emanuel Bach

**Presto**

# Allegro Scherzando

Joseph Haydn
(1732–1809)

## Polonaise

**Moderato**

Wilhelm Friedemann Bach
(1710 – 1784)

# German Dance

**Allegro con brio**

Joseph Haydn

**Trio**

*D. C. al Fine*

# Minuet

Joseph Haydn

poco rit.
a tempo
p
mf
f
crescendo
ff

# Allegro Giocoso

Joseph Haydn
(1732 – 1809)

f
p
f
p
f
mp cresc.
f
mf
p
f
f
mf
p
poco rit.
Da Capo
senza replica

# Viennese Sonatina No. 1

## First Movement

Wolfgang Amadeus Mozart
(1756-1791)

**Allegro brillante**

cresc.

# Minuet and Trio

from Viennese Sonatina No.1

Wolfgang Amadeus Mozart

**Allegretto**

Trio
crescendo
poco rit.
a tempo
Menuetto da capo

# Waltz

Wolfgang Amadeus Mozart
(K.567, No. 5)

# Bagatelle

(Op. 119, No. 11)

Ludwig van Beethoven
(1770–1827)

**Andante ma non troppo**

# Bagatelle

(Op. 119, No. 5)

Ludwig van Beethoven

non legato
crescen-
-do
mf
più f
non legato
f
p subito
pp

# Six Variations On A Swiss Song

Theme

**Andante con moto**

Ludwig van Beethoven

Var. I

Var. II
mf
mf
mf
f
Var. III
Minore
sempre
p e legato
p
mp
p
pp

Var. IV
Maggiore
f
legato
f
mf
f
Var. V
p
sempre dolce
mp
mf

Var. VI
R.H.
dim.

# Three Ländler

Franz Schubert
(1797–1828)

mf
mf
f
3
p
mp
8
f
p
f
8
p

# Five Ecossaises

Franz Schubert

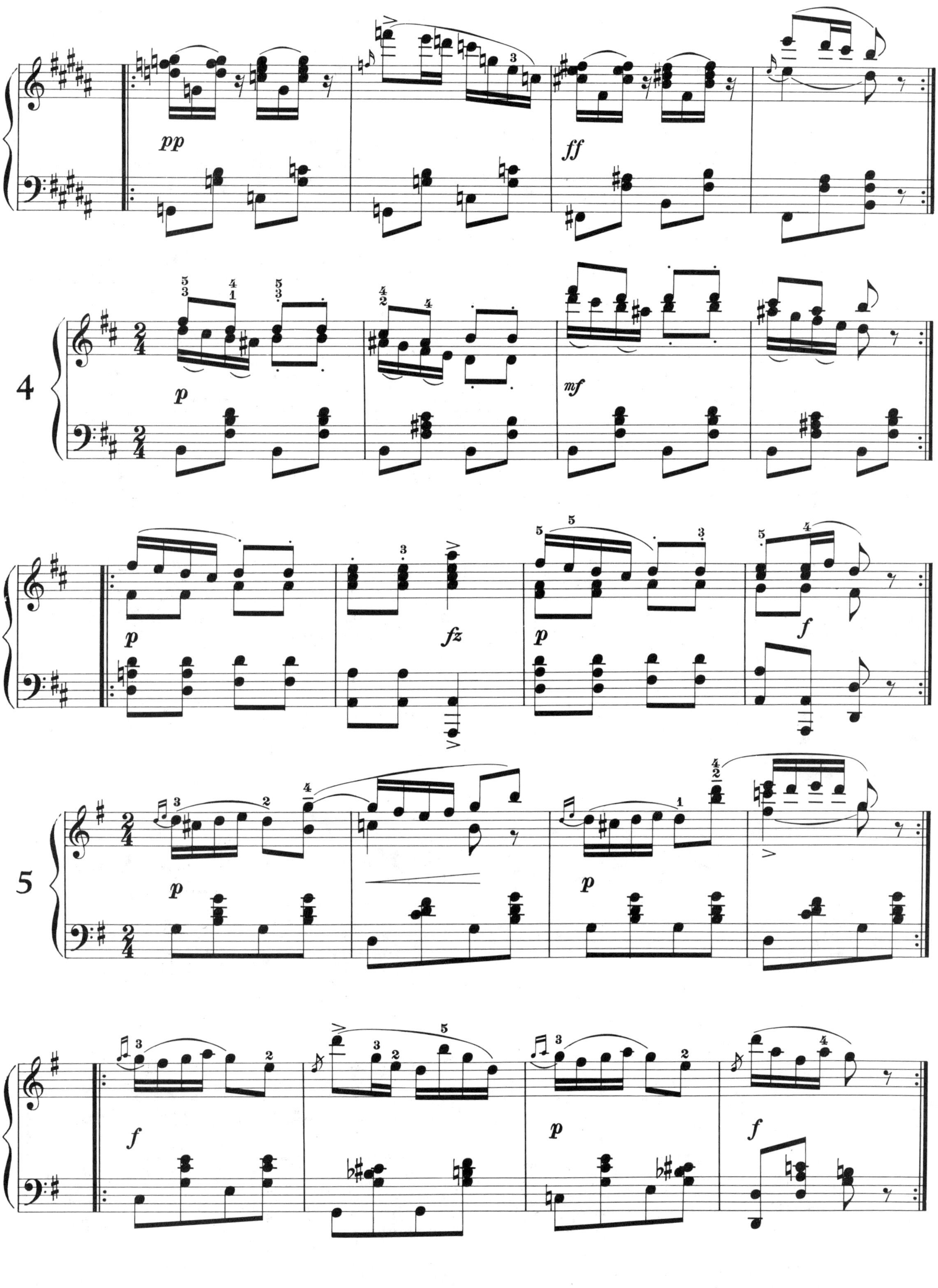
pp
ff
4
p
mf
p
fz
p
f
5
p
p
f
p
f

# Three Waltzes

Franz Schubert

Vivo
3
p
p
mf
1.
2.

# About Strange Lands and People

Robert Schumann
(1810 -1856)

**Andantino**

# Norse Song

## Greeting to G*

Robert Schumann

* *Niels W. Gade, friend of Schumann*

# Rustic Song

Robert Schumann

**Moderato**

# Improvisation*

Robert Schumann

* *On a theme-fragment by Beethoven (Prison Terzett from "Fidelio")*

# Scherzo

Johann Nepomuk Hummel
(1787 - 1837)

**Allegro con brio**

p
p
crescendo
f
dimin.
poco rit.
a tempo
p
mf
crescendo
f
mf
dim. sempre
p
poco accel.
pp
pp

# Children's Piece

(Op. 72, No. 1)

Felix Mendelssohn
(1809-1847)

crescendo
dim.

# Song Without Words

(Op. 19, No. 4)

Felix Mendelssohn

mf
p
rfz
p
crescendo
ff
dim.
ritard.
p
a tempo
pp
p

# Prelude

(Op. 28, No. 6)

Frédéric Chopin
(1810-1849)

# Prelude

(Op. 28, No. 7)

Frédéric Chopin

# Prelude

(Op. 28, No. 4)

Frédéric Chopin

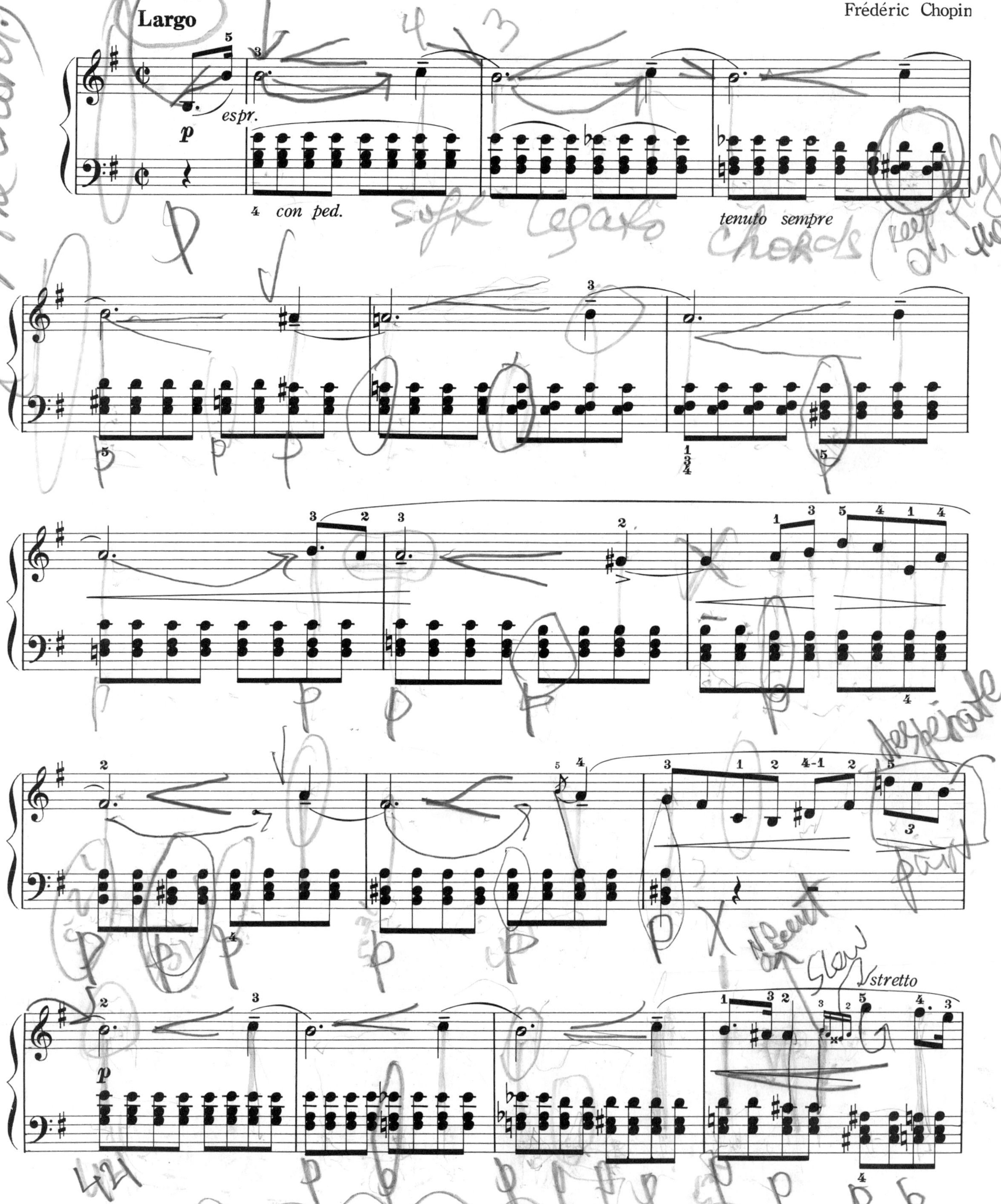

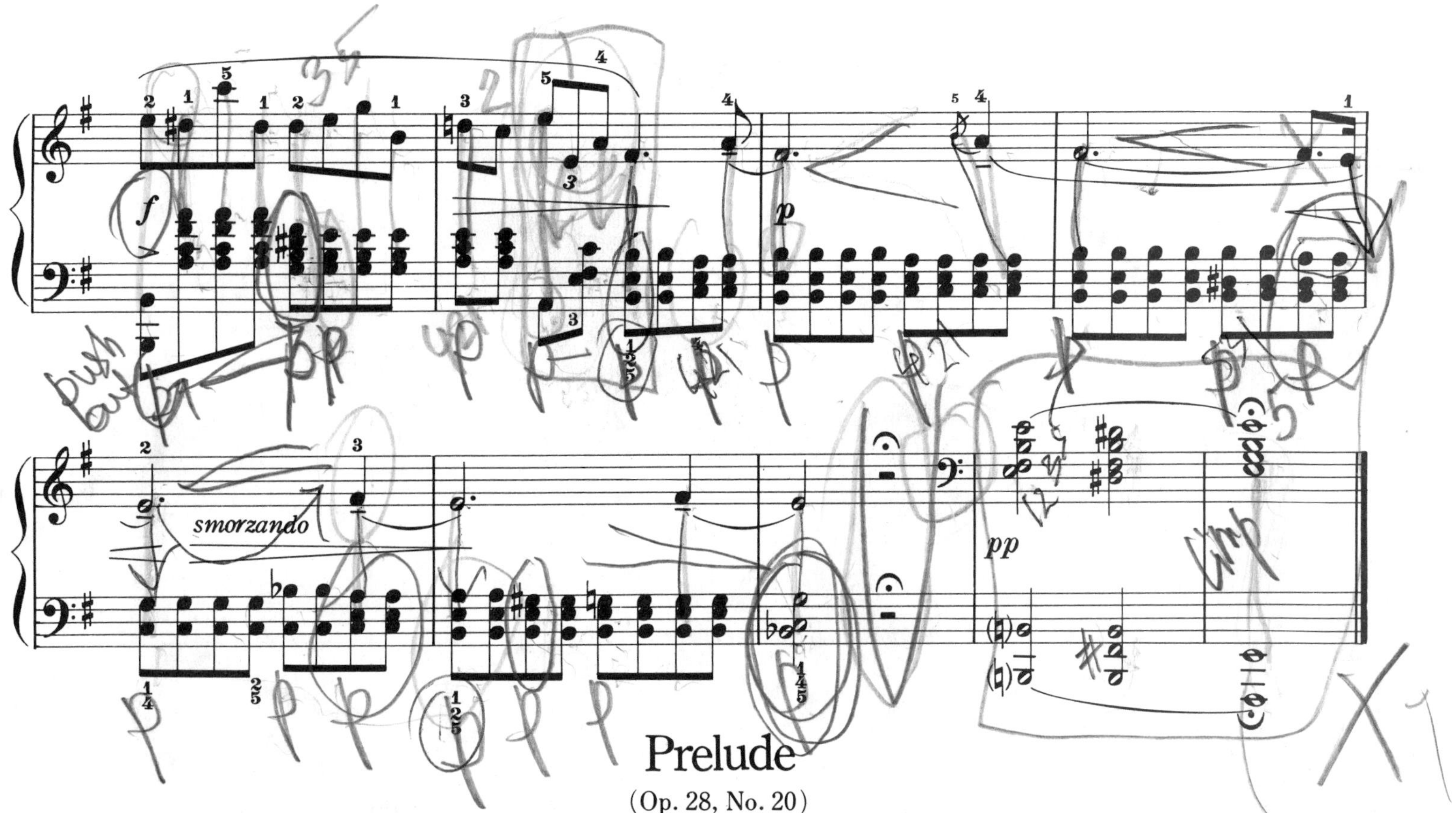


# Prelude

(Op. 28, No. 20)

Frédéric Chopin

**Largo**

# Mazurka

(Op. 67, No. 2)

Frédéric Chopin,

8va
poco cresc.
Tempo I
poco rit.
cresc.
poco rit.

# Tarantella

Michael Glinka
(1804-1857)

**Allegretto**

p legato
pp
mf
p
pp
f
p
f
poco rit.
D. C.

# Waltz

(Op. 39, No. 9)

Johannes Brahms
(1833-1897)

# Album Leaf

César Franck
(1822–1890)

**Allegretto delicato**

# Kamarinskaia

(Russian Folk Tune)

Peter Ilyitch Tchaikovsky
(1840-1893)

# Polka

Peter Ilyitch Tchaikovsky

# Waltz

Peter Ilyitch Tchaikovsky

# Intermezzo

Theodor Kirchner
(1823-1903)

# The Cowherd's Song

(from Op. 17)

Edvard Grieg
(1843-1907)

# Song Of The North

(Saebygga)

(from Op. 17)

Edvard Grieg

# Elfin Dance

Edvard Grieg

fz
f
pp
f
pp
cresc.
f
pp
pp
fz
pp
ppp

# From A Story Book

Robert Volkmann
(1815-1883)

**Allegro giocos**

poco rit.
a tempo
p
crescendo
f
mf
crescendo sempre
f
rit.
dim.

# Valses Poeticos

Enrique Granados
(1867–1916)

## Allegro humoristico

Allegretto elegante
3
f R.H.
mf
p rit.
f a tempo
p rit.
a tempo
f
Fine
p
simile
1.
2.
rall.
rall.
D.C. al Fine

Quasi ad libitum (sentimental)
4
p
con ped.
ten.
rall.
pp
p
a tempo

dim.
poco rall.
pp
mf a tempo
pp
mf
cresc.
con passione
dim.
ten.
p
f con molto espressione
decresc.
mp
rall.
mf a tempo
dim.
p rall. molto

# To A Wild Rose

from " Woodland Sketches"

Edward MacDowell
(1861-1908)

**With simple tenderness**

a tempo
f
diminish
rit.
p
p
mp slightly marked
p
pp
ppp

# Sea Piece

("A merry song, a chorus brave...")

**Lively, in changing moods**

Edward MacDowell

rit.
a tempo
pp
Somewhat slower
pp
f
passionately
rit.
a tempo
pp
slightly rit.
Slower, with great tenderness
mf
dim.
pp

a tempo
f
f
passionately
pp
Tempo I°
crescendo
pp

boisterously
ff
rit.
ff
pp
rit.
Slower, with great tenderness
pp
a tempo
pp
rit.
dim.
ppp

# Frolic

(Op. 17, No. 12)

Max Reger
(1873-1916)

**Allegro vivace**

poco a poco dim. e rit.

a tempo
crescendo

# Dance With A Bell

Vladimir Rebikoff
(1866-1920)

# Kukla

## The Russian Doll

Vladimir Rebikoff

# Prelude No.4

(Op. 11, No. 4)

Alexander Scriabine
(1872-1915)

# Chanson Sans Paroles

(Op. 40, No. 2)

Jan Sibelius
(1865 – 1957)

**Andantino**

mp
p
crescendo
p
dolce
p
dim.

# Romance

Reinhold Glière
(1875-1956)

**Tranquillo**

cresc.
f
dim.
rit.
a tempo
p
mf
dim.
rit.
p

# Gymnopedie No. 3

Erik Satie
(1866 – 1925)

**Lento e grave**

p
L.H.
L.H.
p
pp L.H.
pp

# Brisk Game

Dmitri Kabalevsky
(1904- )

**Allegro assai e marcato**

cresc.
f
f
p
poco a poco cresc.
ff
sf
sf

# Novelette

Dmitri Kabalevsky

look at the music !!
Learn this page separately and together with music!!
sempre cresc.
chromatique base
2 big climax
ff
mf
listen to it
p
pp
p
pp
rit. e dim. al fine
ppp

# The Horseman

Dmitri Kabalevsky

**Allegro molto**

cresc.

# Prelude

Dmitri Shostakovich
(1906- )

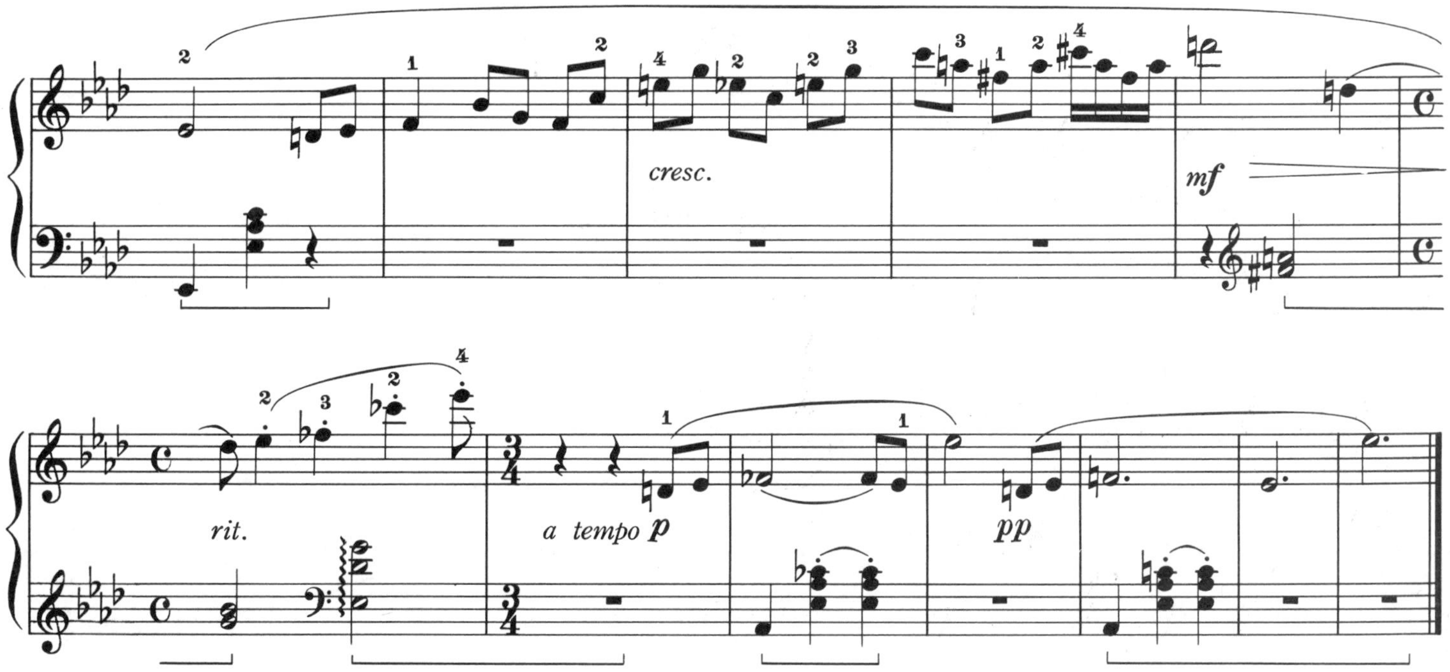


# Parade Of The Grasshoppers

Serge Prokofieff
(1891-1953)

**Allegro**

poco meno mosso
cresc.
mf
p
mp
p
f

dim.
poco rit.
Tempo I
p
cresc.
p
mf
f

# Two Brazilian Children's Songs
from "Guia Prático"

## 1. Farmers' Daughters

Heitor Villa-Lobos
(1881-1959)

2. Goodness!

# Fun At Home

from "The Adventures of Ivan"

Aram Khatchaturian
( 1903- )

# Ivan Is Ill

from "The Adventures of Ivan"

Aram Khatchaturian

**Lento espressivo**

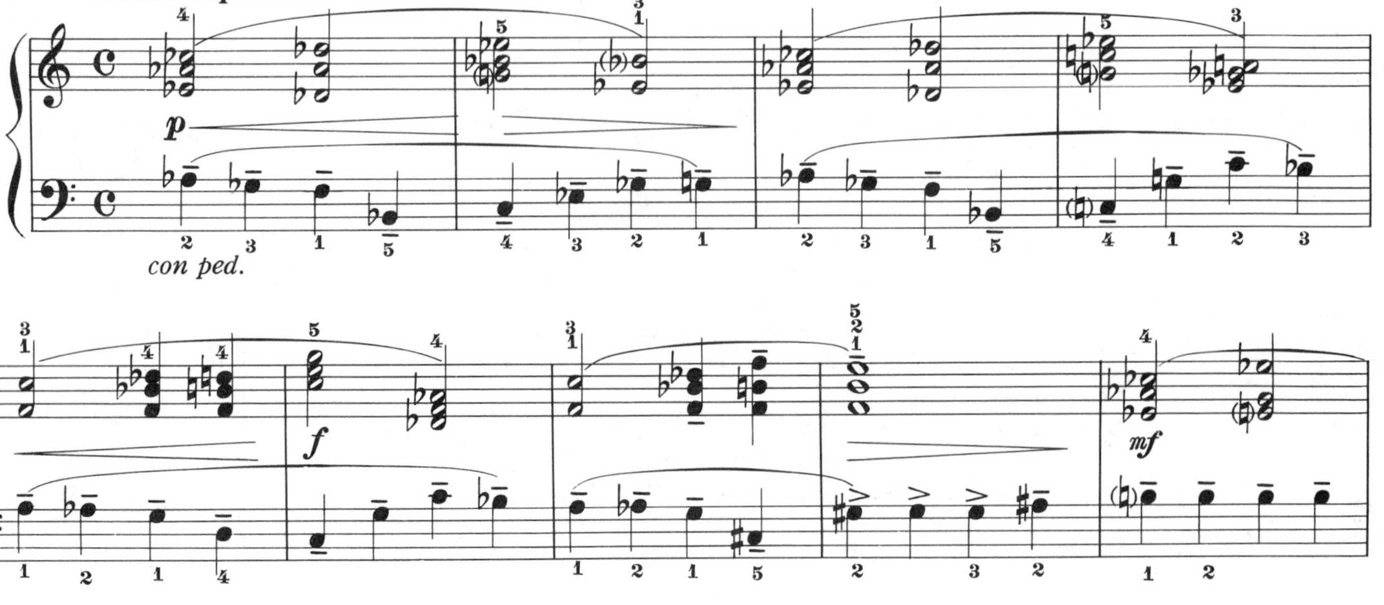

# On The Playground

Nikolai Rakov
(1908- )

**Allegro con brio**

f
mf
dim.
p
mf
p
rit.
f

# Lament

Zoltán Kodály
(1882- )

# Four Hungarian Folk Tunes

## 1.Courting Song

Béla Bartók
(1881-1945)

## 2. Play Tune

Allegro
f
sempre legato
f grazioso
poco cresc.
dim.
p rit.
sempre legato
mf a tempo

f
p
p dolce
poco rit.
mp
a tempo
cresc. sempre
rit.
f
a tempo
p
ritenuto
p

## 3. Stars, Shine Brightly

**Andante sostenuto**

## 4. Drinking Song

# Dawn

Béla Bartók